The Mindful Parent

By Nathalie Perlman

സസസ

© 2013 PJ15 Publishing

All rights reserved. No part of this publication may be reproduced, distributed, or transmitted in any form or by any means, including photocopying, recording, or other electronic or mechanical methods, without the prior written permission of the publisher, except in the case of brief quotations embodied in critical reviews and certain other noncommercial uses permitted by copyright law. For permission requests, write to the publisher, addressed "Attention: Permissions Coordinator," at the address below.

Published by PJ15 Publishing

info@pj15.com

For Jimmy

Index

Preface 6

What is Mindful Parenting 10

    Self-Awareness... 12

    Consciousness without Action 14

    Taking All Cues.. 15

    Focus On Positive Emotions 16

    Constructive Engagement............................ 17

    Compassion Underlines Efforts 18

    Flexibility and Responsiveness 18

    Self-Regulation... 19

Benefits of Being a Mindful Parent 20

    Less Stress.. 20

    More Joy and Satisfaction 21

    Improved Self-Image of Parents 22

    Superior Parenting Skills............................. 23

    Positive and Healthy Parent-Child Relationship 24

    Advantages Children 26

How Does A Parent Become a Mindful Parent? 30

    Become Aware of YOU, first. 30

- Meditation 32
- Journaling 34
- Guided Imagery 36
- Doing the Right Thing in the Moment 37
- Learn to Manage Your Own Stress 39
- Detaching From Your Responses and/or Feelings 39
- How Do I Breathe? 42
- What Does My Body Language Say? 43
- Becoming Aware of How You React, Then Reprogramming 45

The 5 Step Mindful Parent Practice 50

- Stop Whatever you are Doing 50
- Breathe Deep Breaths and Slow Down 52
- Embrace Your Child: Hold Hands, Touch their Head, Give Hugs 53
- Open Your Senses: Observe Your Child's Cues 54
- Enjoy!!! 56

You're Still the Parent 57

- Discipline without Anger 58
- Fences That Stretch and Those That Do Not 60
- The Power of Good and Bad Choices 61
- The Reality of Enjoying Trying Versus Winning 62

Preface

The cold and hard fact about parenting is that it is hard. No matter how you grew up, chances are your parents' skills and advice is not as applicable to today's child as they were then. In fact, your parents probably never had to beg you to get some fresh air, but instead had to fight you to make it home before dark. Kids today are different, and require more resources to entertain and provide for than their parents ever could. This skewed ideology from what worked with your parents to what works now is part of the contentious nature parents and children observe these days. Let's face it: No one ever paid for you to go to the mall at your leisure AND purchase clothing. You were too busy working for a living, delivering newspapers or babysitting to worry about hanging out with your friends. Therein lies the rub. Your parents were parents, and they never cared for one second what you thought about their approach. Now days, that type of parenting does not exist – and in some cases, absolutely shouldn't. That's what being a mindful parent is about. It is sharing your child's experiences, instead of acting as if you are charged with their care until the day they finally move out. It is experiencing the joys and heartaches of childhood with them, instead of glazing over and tuning them out each time they tell a story. It is being involved, and mindful of their livelihood and not just their existence. Mindful parenting allows moms and dads to live in the now, and act upon current situations, instead of dwelling on how terrible of a teacher your child had last year. It is no longer relevant, and not something you need to keep reminding your entire household existed. When you live in the now, it allows your children to understand that their needs are being met in the present – and not focusing on other aspects of life. It allows them to feel a particular connection to you, their environment, home and support group, promoting comfort and enjoyment at all times.

Since change is an inherent segment of everyone's lives, being a mindful parent allows you to help your child(ren) to take stock in their current state. Where you live, where you work, and how both of those important segments of life affect your child's well-being. If you allow stress from work to follow you home, and immediately yell at your child that what you're doing is more important than the A they receive in math today – well, you are doing it wrong – at least from a mindful parenting standpoint.

As parents, it is easy to believe that your life and happiness is more important than that of a child, because you are the one who pays for everything around them, including the video game console that they can hardly be peeled away from. When these feelings are pushed towards the forefront and reflected in your attitude towards your child, they are going to take exception to it in some form. Whether they begin zoning out when you talk, and ignoring what you say altogether, or begin to feel unimportant or alienated, judgement and harsh approaches to parenting will only lead to upsetting behaviour on the part of the child. They are going to begin distancing themselves from their parents, for fear of being judged or scolded, and sooner are later are going to reach out for attention in all the wrong ways.

By incorporating mindfulness to the parenting process, it is possible to enrich the responsibility of being a father or mother and create the potential to reconnect with your children before they begin robbing banks as a result of your previous consternation. When practiced with intention and consistency, mindful parenting helps foster a deeper openness, allowing communication to flow effortlessly between the child and his or her parents, cementing a strong bond within the home. This strength will carry through as your child moves on to college or a career, and will allow them to ask for advice along the way while maintaining an honest and open relationship with you, thanks to the previous solidification of the relationship throughout their childhood.

What is Mindful Parenting

Mindful parenting is considered a conscious effort to raise children with a deep understanding of their positions in life. This on-going process begins when they are infants by portraying trust, compassion and selflessness when they are the most vulnerable. It continues as they are toddlers, and are learning behavioural instincts by watching their parents care for them with a mentoring passion, instead of an authoritative or prejudicial attitude.

This approach brings forth a mutual trust as the child begins interacting with you and others, while procuring a sustained respect that creates a beneficial relationship for both parties. Simply put, your child understands that they have your attention, and that you have theirs when you are interacting with one another. You are not distracted or working on seven different things at once. You are simply listening to your child tell you about their day.

Parents understand the challenges of raising children while maintaining a career, a home and caring for the rest of their obligations at once. This is where mindful parenting becomes so important. Experiencing the present moment, and enjoying the child who is in front of you without worrying about your meeting the next day is paramount to any other obligation you currently have. When your child knows that they have your attention, in that very moment, they are able to talk to you openly and honestly, without feelings of shame or embarrassment. Knowing that you are completely focused on their well-being provides a safe haven of enlightenment that they will carry with them throughout life. If you think back to your childhood or simply consider another parent's personal style when interacting with their kids, you may be overwhelmed with visions of forceful inclusions in soccer or baseball teams, piano lessons or dance classes. We have all seen the child who would rather be at home reading a book than he would on the pitch wearing a jersey, but is there nonetheless because his parents have decided that is what's best for him. This parental approach typically does not end there, and continues throughout the child's life with school, extra-curricular activities and entertainment outlets. This approach will not go unnoticed by the child, and will typically lead to rebelling practices or his reclusion from the parent's involvement later in life. These parents involvement in their child's life will be viewed as a negative approach, and thereby one that needs to be escaped, not enjoyed, by the child in question.

Conversely, mindful parenting significantly differs from common parenting practices. Mindful parenting focuses on the development of self-awareness and the conscious attachment that prevents negativity from taking over the parent-child relationship. Mindful parents create a satisfying relationship with their children based on mutual trust, admiration and reciprocation.

The following discernible features make mindful parenting different from usual parenting processed witnessed in day-to-day lives.

Self-Awareness

A mindful parent has the ability to be totally focused on what is happening in the moment. This allows the mindful parent to listen, understand, accept and productively interact with children considering their individual persona. A high level of awareness among the parents sets the tone for the mindful parenting process. This awareness is visible at two levels, first the parent becomes self-conscious of his emotions, limitations, and expectations and second, the same make-up as it refers to their children. Being in a mindful state of consciousness prevents strong emotions from overwhelming the parent-child relationship and brings in more trust. Further parents become more aware of the uniqueness each child is endowed with, and they stay committed to remain non-judgmental allowing the child to grow depending on his ability and learning capacity. Accordingly they also develop parenting skills and abilities that allow them to show compassion towards children while remaining sensitive to their needs and aspirations. A mindful parent respects the uniqueness of each child and protects it in thought and action. Both parent and child have distinct personalities and require two completely different growth trajectories. Parents with more than one child recognize the distinct personalities of each and develop parenting skills suitable for each child separately.

Consciousness without Action

A mindful parent is aware without allowing feelings of judgment, defense or other responses to kick in while they are receiving "information" from their child. Simply put, if you were more of a self-proclaimed "nerd" when you were younger, it is not fair to roll your eyes at your child when she proclaims that she wants to try out for the cheerleading squad. Just because it was never your "thing" does not mean it cannot be hers. Mindful parenting is the application of this approach when listening to your children's wants and desires. Instead of enacting your biases and desires, listen to their desires clearly and support their decisions completely.

Mindful parenting involves non-judgmental acceptance of yourself and your child. Though parents are expected to offer guidance and enact discipline, mindfulness prevents them from doing so in an unnecessary manner. There is absolutely no need to offer guidance or judgment if your child wants to become a cheerleader. All you have to do is understand her emotional excitement and feed it with support.

Likewise, if you were the cheerleader in school, and your child shows no interest in the same, it is important to provide a giant smile and supportive hoorah when she comes home and wants to be captain of the debate club. Support the child you have, not the one you want them to be.

Taking All Cues

A mindful parent is absorbing their child's words, tone, facial expressions, body language and other cues, going beyond simply hearing words they say. Parents remain sensitive to the content of the conversations, effectively using these cues to successfully detect your child's needs or intended meanings. Such detailed attention allows parents to develop a reflective capacity that helps understand and link child's physical, emotional and psychological state to their own. This allows parents to understand children in a better way, analyse their temperament and feelings more accurately and reduce conflict and disagreement. By doing so parents can promote positivity in the relationship by helping the child understand that they are truly listening and have utmost care and support for his physical or emotional comfort.

Focus On Positive Emotions

Positive emotions are the core of mindful parenting. When you interact with your child in a positive way, especially when it comes to their negative complaints or emotions, it will help them understand that remaining open-minded and accepting is the better path to happiness. If they are upset that they are going to be late to the party, remind them that they will get to put their gift on the top of the pile, which will make it first in line for opening. If your child becomes emotional due to the behaviour of another child, remind them that it is important to show others how to share and be nice to one another. It is important to remain positive, even when you think they are not looking or listening. If you are in the car, do not explode with negativity at the sight of traffic. This will lead them to believe that it is okay to criticize happenings that are out of your control.

Do not project unrealistic expectations upon your child by being negative about circumstances whether they concern them or not.

Constructive Engagement

Mindful parenting persuades parents to withhold strong emotions while interacting with children and ensure more consciousness to influence the relationship. This means helping your child build a castle the way they dreamed it would be, and not how you want it to stand. This also means helping them get dressed in the clothes they picked out, without reminding them that another shirt would match their pants better. Engaging your child should bring a smile to their faces, and not a sense of retracting. If you start towards your kid's room, and he immediately pulls away, you are not being constructive – you are bullying him. Constructive engagement is the act of approaching your child with happiness and excitement, so that they know the first thing that comes out of your mouth is going to be a welcomed, loving statement. You do not have to take control of any situation they are in, you simply have to sit beside him and let him tell you what is happening and how you can help.

Compassion Underlines Efforts

Active concern and compassion for children is an essential dimension of mindful parenting. Mindful parents showcase a greater sense of positive affection, acceptance and support towards their children. When your child knows that you truly care about his or her well-being, and that you are listening with compassion, than he knows that he can tell you anything at any time.

Flexibility and Responsiveness

Mindful parenting focuses on greater parental flexibility and effective responsiveness. Let your child know that you can bend with the occasion, and circumvent the rules to get the most desired result for their well-being. That does not mean that you will lie to get them into the best schools, it just means that you will leave work a little early to make it to their recital, even though they know you are very dedicated to your career. Being a responsive parent means knowing when your child needs you, and dropping anything else to ensure they are getting the best advice possible the very moment that they need it.

Self-Regulation

Self-control and self-regulation are two key attributes of a mindful parent. Greater awareness allows parents to become conscious of their limitations, abilities and emotions to address their feelings and mind set at the present time. Their superior ability to understand and accept differing situations, personalities and conditions helps them refrain from displaying a negative response, such as anger or hostility, and empowers them to remain constructive. They are empowered to select better parenting practices, instead of letting their emotions get the best of them. This measured response by mindful parents promotes goodwill among children and aids in their socializing.

Benefits of Being a Mindful Parent

Mindful parenting, when practiced with intention and consistency, empowers parental skills and fosters a superior parent-child relationship. It ensures better flow of communication, stress-free parenting, improved awareness and a better environment for self-growth of children.

The following are the key benefits of mindful parenting.

Less Stress

Parents feel the pinch of stress when the expectations they have from their child fail to materialise. They come to consider their parenting skills inadequate and the parenting process a failure. In many cases, the stress causes them to consider their children a failure. Mindful parenting offers an escape from this stress. Mindful parents remain compassionate, considerate, unselfish and realistic in their anticipations. They do not expect much from the child to satisfy their own expectations.

Their altruistic attitude helps them remain unselfish and they do not push children for goals conceived at parental level.

In this way, parents can be freed from the egoistic, habitual, and hedonic motivations that may lead them astray in their parenting practices and cultivate a parenting perspective that incorporates a long view of the enduring nature of the relationship with the use of wisdom in selecting appropriate parenting responses in the moment. They do not remain anxious for their failure to understand children's activities. Absence of expectation and no feelings of embarrassment lead to no stress.

More Joy and Satisfaction

A higher level of mindfulness leads to lower levels of depressive symptoms and stress. Parents do not see child behaviour problems in comparison to what they have learned so far in their lives. Their awareness of their own limitations and that of their children ensures that they do not have unrealistic expectations for their child. The altruistic nature of mindful parenting keeps them happy with their efforts and they do not strive to achieve unnecessary targeted objectives during the parenting process.

Mindful parenting draws out and strengthens the inner capacities of parents; it is not simply a new skill set, but rather a different way of thinking, perceiving and knowing. The close relationship that derives from this between parents and children ensures better interaction and parents feel the joy of being close to their children. They relish in their ability of becoming a good father or mother who provide the best possible health, happiness and success for their children.

Improved Self-Image of Parents

The following six factors contribute to the improved self-image of mindful parents.

- No stress
- Enhanced awareness level
- Better parenting skills
- Ability to foster better relationships with children
- Positive home environment
- Ability to have constructive engagement

Stress in parenting leads to distraction and dysfunction in other personal and professional responsibilities. As the parenting process is smooth and joyful, it aids in better motivation and success across the spectrum of activities. The high level of self-awareness attained by mindful parents helps them evaluate their own abilities and improve them. They acquire new skills to fulfil the needs of their children.

Mindful parents are an example for all and even elevate their social standing, by having a good relationship with their children. Their efforts to become better parents also cause behavioural changes in other areas of life like social interactions on the street or at the office. They prefer to shun addiction, violence and strong emotions. The improved ability to creatively engage with children ensures new ways of thinking and better skills to navigate and mediate challenges.

Superior Parenting Skills

Mindful parenting leads to a fundamental shift in the psychology and ability of parents. They become keen to be truly present with the constantly growing child and ready to acquire parenting skills required to foster and support the changing nature of their child. The willingness to better their relationship with children makes them to participate in parenting workshops, devise new methods, and remain more attentive to child's needs and work to fulfil their requirements. Conscious parents feel it as their obligation to provide all possible support to their children to become bona fide members of society without sacrificing their unique identity. They progressively adopt practices that can help understand the unique nature of their children and benefit in their physical, cognitive and psychological developments. Empathy and compassion make their interventions positive in nature. Such parents are ready to run the extra mile for their children and save them from any kind of distress.

Positive and Healthy Parent-Child Relationship

Mindful parenting allows you to have a more epistemological orientation which takes the strain out of the parent-child relationship. Better communication and altruistic parenting helps create and maintain a relationship devoid of expectations or biased view. Deeper understanding of a child's feelings and sensitivity makes parents more realistic and guide them successfully whenever required. It also minimizes the need for intervention, prevent sweeping emotions and create a more amenable environment for constructive and fruitful parent-child engagement.

Parental ability to listen to their children's voice and read their emotions ensures that there is no rough ride for them. They are able to convey their approvals without any interventionist attitude. Positive relationship with their children empowers parents with a sense of optimism. This gives them the inner strength and skills to mitigate some of the individual, family, neighbourhood and societal factors that put children and youth at risk. Young people are then less likely to develop serious problems that can diminish their well-being and opportunities at school and in the community. They develop resilience and a flexible posture within their world.

Advantages Children

The way parents interact with kids impacts all aspects of childhood development, including the way children respond to situations and the world around them. Mindful parenting is an effective medium to learn to live in the moment and bring mindful qualities, including curiosity, acceptance, observation and non-judgment to the parent-child relationship. Mindfulness enables parents to enrich their connection with their kids. Research has proved that children enjoying a strong connection with their parents and living in a stress-free environment - replete with calm, peace, acceptance and love - have higher self-esteem, feel comfortable around adults, choose healthy relationships, explore new things, do better in school and readily adapt to changes.

- Greater parental attention leads to better understanding of the child's behaviour and requirements. Parents do everything likely to support their children and secure them from distress. Assured attention and support from parents encourages children to achieve their full potential on their own without any fear or obstruction.

- Superior parental understanding of the child's emotions allows them to bring in quality upbringing and guide him constructively. Parental empathy cultivates a parenting perspective that incorporates a long view of the enduring nature of the relationship with the use of wisdom in selecting appropriate parenting responses in the moment.
- Better communication between parents and child fosters a positive environment. They understand each other in a better way and remain close. It also prevents strong emotions to wreck the relationship or making parents biased against the child.
- No parental expectations and self-regulation allows more liberty for children. They can determine their qualities, acquire skills, and develop inner strength with full support from parents. There is no pressure on them to go after any particular objective they are not competent for and experience failure.

- Full respect of child's unique personality means due parental consideration and respect for children. No push to proceed according to the planned itinerary, strenuously trying to make life conform to parent needs, or adapt to whatever children cannot meet and flow.
- Consciousness of present time keeps old traditions and values that can impinge the children's choices. This also allows parents to change and progressively adopt new skills for the betterment of their child.
- Altruist attitude make parents to showcase unselfish concern for the welfare of children. They remain non-judgemental and likely to support children in efforts befitting their personality and skills.
- Non-intervention by mindful parents allows children freedom from stress and psychological reactivity. They are allowed to grow and develop on their own with parental care and support. However, limited intervention assists in course correction and conduct control and

this is reflective of parents' wish for wellbeing of children rather than their own selection.

- Positive parent-child relationship achieved through mindful parenting fosters a better environment at home and allows both to relish in their success. The mutual trust plays a crucial role in guiding children during their teen age.

How Does A Parent Become a Mindful Parent?

Psychologist and mindfulness researcher Dr. Pearce has succinctly summed up the fundamental core of the relationship between parents and children, saying *"Nature designed us to love our children and allow them to love us. Love is the safe-space, in which both parent and child can play and where learning takes place naturally. A parent can't teach love. They can only love and the child's natural state unfolds in response to that love. A parent can't love if he or she was never loved when they were children. But the natural state of a child will teach the parent to love in turn, if the parent is tuned in to that child".*

Become Aware of YOU, first.

The first step to mindful parenting is to become self-aware by bringing more attentiveness to your body and mind. It is important to understand whether you are overreacting or responding negatively to a given situation simply because you have had a bad day. After assessing the situation you are able to respond more mindfully and come up with a nuanced, spacious and unique outcome. You can then begin to start questioning the reality of your statements. When you experience self-awareness, it helps bring out another dimension of the experience. If you learn to become aware of your breathing and sustain it for a long time, it can be a very powerful experience and provide a calming, concentrated affect to a seemingly hostile situation. Whether we respond mindfully or react mindlessly, it will impact our child.

Mindful parenting is about learning to slow things down and observing your reactions, rather than pushing for an immediate action on behalf of your kids. This will help you effectively restructure your family's routine. It is okay for the kids to be their own person, and project that through their clothing, hair styles and actions. Allow them to use their own creativity and imagination as they grow and discover who they are, and what they like. It is important to place ourselves in their shoes and try to understand their mind set and point of view. We cannot expect our children to think the way we do – their thoughts are certainly going to be different from that of ours at such a tender age. They are also going to change their stance on life no less than one thousand times before they leave high school, so it is important for you to grow WITH them, not against them along the way.

Meditation

Step out of your emotional reactions, judgments and internal assumptions and note how they oppress or limit your parenting skills. Take a few deep mini-awareness breaths and stop what you are doing and reflect on everything happening in life. Observe who influences your life, including the people and events for which you are grateful. Focus on the emotions, thoughts, feelings and sensations that arise within as you partake in daily activities, including working in the garden, folding laundry, washing dishes, or performing mundane tasks. Think about the animals, people and issues that you are most concerned about and visualise and direct feelings of kindness toward them.

Meditation for mindful parenting teaches you effective breathing, relaxation and visualisation techniques that will help you control emotions, manage stress, and face the challenges of parenting with joy, calm and focused energy.

Meditation techniques will help you:

- Shift your Perspective to What's Important
- Helps You Forgive and Forget the Little Things
- Accept the Present Moment & That Some Things Are Out of Your Control
- Focus on Inner Peace & Stillness
- Generate Kindness, Especially Towards Your Children
- Acknowledge & Understand Your Child's World and Behaviours

As a mindful parent, you learn to become aware of your kids needs and desires, and your ability to relate to them. At the same time, it is important to observe your internal world and develop mindfulness that can enhance your relationship with your children. Meditation enables you to explore how taking care of yourself helps you take better care of your children and become a more thoughtful, focused and committed parent.

Mindful parenting simply requires you to be human. There is no magic potion, or spell that you can cast on your home, you simply have to realize that your responses and interactions with your child can always be kind and observant. When you pay attention to your inner thoughts and feelings, you are able to bring awareness to any outside forces affecting your body. This can include stress, tension or even physical anxiety. Ask yourself whether you are really worried about solving an issue, or if you are simply obsessing about it in an unhealthy manner.

When you tune into your breathing, and the sensations that encompass it, you are learning to step outside of time and invite calmness within. Mindfulness is a practice that saves you considerable time and allows you to reclaim your moments as they are happening.

Journaling

Begin creating a journal to note your inner and outer responses to life and the different situations that present themselves. There isn't a better way to improve mindfulness than journaling. You can vividly learn to live each moment with self-awareness, presence, attentiveness and heart-centred compassion within yourself. Journaling does not mean you are keeping a diary. It is meant to encourage creative expression and self-growth through storytelling, doodling or even making lists of things you plan to do in life. It helps you develop a focus on your inner world, while reducing negativity. It also allows you to get a number of items off your chest and onto paper, so you can let them go. Journaling is a mindful check-in that does not require any kind of special equipment and can be done anywhere. It allows you to close your eyes and reflect on all the things that are going on within your head and heart, before opening the journal expressing these sentiments into a stream of consciousness by simply thinking "What am I feeling right now?" Experts believe that even one journaling session can be life-changing, while regular practice can increase self-awareness, mindfulness, self-efficacy, wellness and personal growth. Journaling can be straight-forward, cryptic, in pictures or simply words piled onto paper, delivering a deeper sense of emotional clarity while improving your sense of self.

Mindful journaling can help you:

- Release Anger, Tension, Frustration & Strong Emotions
- Find your Creative Voice
- Tap into Your Subconscious Knowledge and Wisdom
- Experiment with Creative Writing
- Clarify Personal Goals
- Become More Present in the Moment
- Become Less Judgmental Toward Yourself & Others
- Keep a Written Record of the Days Gone By
- Treat your Journal as a Trusted Friend & Source of Release
- Manifest Your Inner Beauty

Guided Imagery

This method requires you to employ each of your five senses – taste, touch, smell, sound and sight – to visualise something. Breathe deeply and instil the story in your memory. This guided imagery works best in stressful times, especially when you want to become calm. You can begin thinking of your favourite vacation destination while feeling the sand in your toes and smelling the sea water as you hear it bounce against the coast. You can taste an umbrella-laden while watching the sun beam directly onto your face. Relaxed? Of course you are. Use this guided imagery to get you through tough parenting times, so you can make decisions that suit you and your family collectively. No matter how mindful you become, parenting is still a tough job and is going to require some removal from the process from time to time – even if only for a few seconds.

Doing the Right Thing in the Moment

The idea of being a mindful parent is to trust our intuition that we are doing the right thing in the moment. Mindful parenting is about spending time to reflecting on being mindful of our needs and desires, as well as those of your child. It is important that your needs – as an adult, and a parent – are being met in order to effectively meet your children's needs. It is therefore important to allow yourself enough time to connect with your children as well as with yourself, your friends, partner, family and everything else. Mindful parenting is a deeper style of parenting that affects the relational as well as emotional development of the child. It is important to attend to your kids in emotionally present ways, and if you don't, this amounts to disrespecting the basic threads of connectivity between your children and you. Research shows that if parents are emotionally present in a mindful and balanced way, their children are better equipped to deal with emotionally charged situations. A number of studies suggest that kids who feel deeply connected to their parents have higher self-esteem and perform well in school, besides developing a better understanding as to how to socialize and be comfortable around adults. Such children can easily adapt to changes and develop a positive self-concept, resulting in them choosing healthy relationships.

Learn to Manage Your Own Stress

The greatest source of childhood stress is parental stress, not school work, peer pressure, or extracurricular activities. So to be a good parent, you must first learn to manage your own stress and make peace with your imperfections. It is important to learn how to regulate your emotional state and become calmer and present when your kids need your attention.

Detaching From Your Responses and/or Feelings

Having a fight with your spouse or worrying about money should never be things your child has to deal with emotionally. Parents live under the illusion that kids have "no idea" what is happening in their home, even when parents are being snide and awful to each cryptically in front of them. The truth is, children can read your emotions and vibe whether you are upset, sad, or being just plain nasty. They read your tone, facial expressions and temperament, just like you read theirs so it is important to detach from the negativity before interacting with your child.

When stressful workdays accompany you through the door of your home in the evenings, your children can feel the stress from the moment you walk in. Especially if you look frazzled, exhausted, overwhelmed or nonplussed by a recent conversation. If that is the case, as it is for all parents on bad days, it is important for you to detach from the stress before entering the home. If this means you have to take the long way home, and meditate while you are stuck in traffic, so be it.

Your kids are not the source of your stress, and it should never be taken out on them in any form. Whether the form manifests itself by thinking about anything but what they are saying to you, or taking a phone call in the middle of a conversation about their school day. It is important to put it all behind you from the moment you walk in the door, during dinner and through their bedtimes.

At the end of each day, you have the exact same amount of hours on earth as everyone else. It is important that you use that time wisely to respect your children's livelihoods while they are in front of you.

Detaching is not easy, and typically does not come naturally to most parents, so you will have to work on it. A good place to start is by telling your colleagues that you do not answer emails, texts or take phone calls from the time you get home until the moment your kids are in bed. If you choose to immerse yourself back into your work life thereafter, that is your personal choice. In addition, make sure family members understand that everyone is expected to provide each individual in the household with the same amount of respect. No one problem in the home is bigger than another when one child has the floor. Give each their turn, and respect their situations individually before trying to solve one problem in conjunction with another.

Once a family issue is resolved, restart your emotionally involvement to focus solely on the next child's issue, concern, excitement or announcement. It is important to evolve with your family, and detach from everything else when you are interacting with them. This includes sporting events, dance classes and extra-curricular activities. It is unfair to answer emails on your phone at your kid's baseball game. Although he may not be able to see you, you certainly are not there in spirit either, so what's the point? Focus on your children while they are awake and need your support. Everything else can wait.

How Do I Breathe?

Do you have any idea what your breathing says about you? It is probably most noticeable when you are in a tremendous hurry and bustling from train to train or through stairwells to get to a meeting on time. Your panting and quick short breaths will tell everyone on the elevator that you are running late.

When you are stressed, your breathing takes a different turn and sounds burdened and worried. The sigh of angst and exhaustion is audibly displayed – even if you are doing it subconsciously. It is important to be mindful of your breathing by taking a few seconds to listen to it in a quiet space. Close your eyes and allows your breath to go in and out, until it becomes regulated and subdued.

Take the time to listen to yourself breathe when you are at rest, so you know what calm and containment sound like, and remember how you got to that quiet breathing point. Were you thinking of how restful you were or of something you love so dearly? If so, take yourself back to that place when your breath becomes stressed or upset. Your child is not going to want to explain how their day went to you while you are huffing and puffing through the house. Learn to listen to yourself breathe, so you can control it when you need to.

What Does My Body Language Say?

Certainly it is no secret that your body language speaks volumes, even when you are not saying a single word. Whether it is your hands moving up and down with emphasis or standing with your arms folded when you are receiving news you are not excited about, your kids are no fools and are able to read your dismay through your body language.

Although you may have your emotions in check verbally, that does not mean you have mastered the control of your body language. When your child approaches, do you stop what you are doing and place your body facing them, making eye contact? A mindful parent delivers focus and undivided attention to their child when they are delivering news or information.

When parents do so, children follow their lead and will stop playing, running, moving or dancing when they are addressed by their parent to show the same respect in return.

It is important to monitor your body language, and consciously make a decision to improve it when you are talking to your children. Keep in mind that a hand on the hip says "Sure you did" while crossed arms say, "I'm unhappy with your decision making." All of these things can alter the way a child interacts with you, and a mindful parent is aware of that. When your child enters the room and you do not bother turning to face them, you are saying "What you have to say is not important enough to consume my attention." Imagine if someone treated you the same way. And then imagine when they do, that their parents treated them differently and how you are keeping your child from becoming one of those people.

Remember that every sigh, hand wave and gesture you make speaks on your behalf and can damage your child's self-esteem and ability to interact with you in a single approach. Should you find yourself sighing at yet another Science project need resulting in a late night errand to the drug store, your kids are going to forgo asking you for the easy to obtain poster board next time. They will just skip the assignment. When asked why, kids are never shy about sharing their honest feelings, so if it is too much to ask to run to your nearest retailer after dinner, don't worry – they will let the world know.

This is part of the mindful experience. Although you are not talking, you are expressing your feelings through breathing and body language, so it is important to know how those expressions are received by the young people in your home.

Becoming Aware of How You React, Then Reprogramming

Being a parent does not make you a superhero, no matter how much you would like for it to. You cannot simply flip a switch the day your baby comes home from the hospital that says, "I will react to everything in my child's life with care and compassion going forward – no matter what!" It just does not happen that way.

One way of becoming aware of how you react to certain situations is to keep a journal of your emotions throughout the day, or the week. If you yell when you are angry, ask yourself why and really try and get to the root of the cause before your child is old enough to be screamed at when you are stressed or upset. No child deserves to be screamed at, even when your emotions get the best of you, so be mindful of your triggers and handle them with a meditative moment instead of a knee-jerk reaction.

If you emotional state evolves into tears, it is important for you to understand that your child equates crying with sadness. They are not old enough to understand that happiness, surprise and love can all result in tears, so be sure to control those emotions by heading off tearful opportunities when they might arise. For instance, skip a television special about children suffering or abuse victims before you plant to interact with your child.

Mindful parenting means assessing your feelings to insure that they are not going to manipulate the way you raise your child. The goal is to raise a perfectly respectable person, not one who folds at the very sign of adversity simply because you do. If you have ever needed a reason to be strong and work towards maintaining your composure, having a child emulate your actions should be enough to make that happen. When you are assessing your emotional state, ask yourself a few simple questions to help you get the bottom of why your scream, cry or become withdrawn in certain situations. These questions can help you deliver yourself from reactionary status, and reprogram your thinking to provide a more mindful parenting experience for your child.

Keep in mind, if your emotions get the best of you, and you react to your child with guilt, shame, or an upset tone, they are no longer going to come to you with a similar issue. This creates distance between you and your child by pushing an emotional wedge between the two of you. It is more important to note that if that happens, YOU are to blame – not the child.

To help reprogram your reactionary status, ask yourself the following questions and – more importantly – answer them HONESTLY when referring to a particularly emotional situation.

- **First:** How Does that (event, situation, occurrence, news or announcement) Make Me Feel?
- **Second:** Why Does That Make Me Feel That Way?
- **Lastly:** How Would I Rather Feel About It?

Chances are, the answers are going to sound something like "Because it upsets me to see children suffer" and "I wish I was able to show more strength and courage." When you know why a situation or occurrence upsets or angers you, it is up to you as an adult to counter those feelings with emotions you would rather have. This is not going to happen overnight. It is literally a reprogramming process that needs to happen in order for you to share a mindful parenting experience with your child.

Your kids sure certainly understand risk versus reward and consequences and accountability, but they can be taught these valuable experiences by a calm, calculated and communicative parents, instead of one who screams when angered. Things happen, and kids are never going to be perfect angels. However, it is up to you to possess the open mind and the actual inclination to change your reactionary practices to calmer conversations.

The 5 Step Mindful Parent Practice

There are a number of easy steps that you can initiate to become a mindful parent, and help your child communicate with you more openly while discovering the value of shared trust, respect and compassion. These five steps can be learned quickly with a mindful approach to becoming a better parent. Keep in mind that you have always been able to accomplish your goals, and if your latest one is to become a mindful parent, it is worth taking the time to make it happen successfully.

1. Stop Whatever you are Doing

It is no secret that the days move quickly, and that there is so much to do as a parent. You have a home, a career, a family and friends to care for, listen to and take care of. However, a mindful parent understands that their child's needs should come first. The goal of being a mindful parent is to raise a well-adjusted child who respects the world and the people around him. In order to do so, the first thing you must do is stop whatever you are doing and enjoy what is happening in front of you.

When your child approaches you for a chat, an announcement or even a solution, stop what you are doing and look to them with care. Refrain from solving their problems immediately, and allow them to explain their position, predicament or make their announcement. Giving your child time to formulate their own ideas helps them become problem solvers while using you as a sounding board.

When you remain busy or distracted while your child talks to you, your body language is telling them that you do not have time to listen, or that what they are saying is not important enough to stop what you are doing. There is no need to make your child feel slighted. You're busy, and quite honestly so is everyone else. Take the time to indulge your child at every opportunity so they know how important they are to you.

2. Breathe Deep Breaths and Slow Down

When you are hustling around the house, between errands or sporting events, you are passing the world by, undoubtedly with your child in tow. What do you think this teaches them? That there is no time to smile, chat or simply take the world in around you.

When your breathing picks up to a panicked or hurried state, your child feels as if there is no time to point out things that tickle their curiosity. Imagine your child, wondering on his own, "What is that? What does it do? Can I get closer to it?" while you are dragging him frantically through the grocery in an effort to make it to the dry cleaner on time. Kids pick up on this emotional tour and lean to simply keep their questions and observations to themselves.

Mindful parenting means taking the time to insure that your child is fulfilled in society. It certainly is not necessary to move at their pace or you would never get anything accomplished, but it is necessary to encourage their growth through questions and comments. Allow them to take in the world around them, and ask how much things cost, or how dry cleaners operate. Allow them to ask other people their names, or how they are. Wherever you are, SLOW DOWN and allow the small person with you to learn about all of the things you already know and take for granted. How else will they learn?

3. Embrace Your Child: Hold Hands, Touch their Head, Give Hugs

Not enough can be said about how important it is to embrace your child. Sure, once they hit a certain age, they no longer want to kiss you before they start their day, but that doesn't mean you can't encourage them to. When your kids are small, hold their tiny little hands when they talk to you. It provides a clear sense of connection and compassion, allowing them to feel loved even if they are telling you that they broke your favorite vase.

When you are in public, waiting in line or simply communicating with others, hold them close to you by placing your hands on their shoulders, or by touching their head or hair while they talk. They will understand how much you adore them, and it will boost their self-esteem.

Lastly, hug your child every chance you get. Tell them you love them, and that you are proud of them at every turn. You do not have to smother your child, but you can hug them as a greeting and farewell. Kids who are affectionate and friendly are more social and outgoing than those who are not. Hugs are not simply for missing someone, they are for happiness each time you are able to enjoy their company. Teach your child that hugs are not reserved for special occasions.

4. Open Your Senses: Observe Your Child's Cues

Mindful parenting means being aware of your child's emotions, and picking up on their cues along the way. Your child should not have to scream and cry to show you they are upset or hurt by something that has happened. Their cues give away their emotions, and it is up to you as a parent to read them properly. When you start observing your children when they are young, it is easy to pick up on how they react to certain situations. Much like poker players, kids have what are called "tells". This mean they may shift their weight, play with their hair or simply fidget uncontrollably when they are uncomfortable. This is something you should be aware of when your kids are visiting friends, or are in public, as it is their quiet way of saying, "I do not feel safe here."

Smiles are easy to understand, but what about when they are withdrawn? If your kid spends their entire day in their room, while telling you that "nothing is wrong" mindful parents will know better by picking up on their cues. When you kid is not eating, or does not want to go to a certain place or be around certain people it is important that you understand why, instead of dismissing it as nothing.

Mindful parents are able to pick up on their kid's cues when they are unwilling to look them in the eye when asking a question, or when they fall behind in school work. Everything your child does they do for a reason. It can be good or bad, but it is for a purpose. It is up to you as their parent to be mindful enough to know what is happening, while encouraging them through trust and compassion to tell you what that "thing" is.

5. Enjoy!!!

Being mindful does not mean you and your child have to be under a microscope to make sure you are doing it right. Have fun with your kids, and get to know the things they enjoy so you can enjoy them too. If your child loves science, make a game of having them explain it to you. If your daughter loves make-up, let her give you a makeover. Enjoy the time you have with your kids as long as you can, so when they actually have friends that consume most of their time, they know they can always come back to you for the sage advice you have always provided.

Enjoy life with the people you love, and allow everyone in the family to influence the others' actions and adventures. Being well-rounded takes a lot of experience and input from the world around you. Help your child enjoy it as much as they can, before they have to start paying a mortgage.

You Are Still The Parent

Make no mistake: You are still the parent in this relationship. Mindful parenting is no excuse to allow your child to run around a store or house acting like a maniac, simply because it is fun. Mindful parenting is how you communicate with your child, and apply respect and compassion. Part of that respect is teaching them that other people's space, belongings and feelings matter too and should be respected no matter where you are. Mindful parenting is reading your child's actions while you are at home or in public, and engaging them when they need your assistance. It is in no way a license to misbehave, run free or harm others. As a parent, it is up to you to explain risk versus reward, actions versus consequences, proper communication skills, respect, compassion, sharing and caring. You child needs to know that if someone is talking, they are to wait their turn. If another child is playing with a toy, they cannot rip it from their hands and take over. If an adult asks them to stop running through their home, they should stop. Mindful parenting is part of an overall awareness of your child's well-being and livelihood – not a free for all to let your child do whatever he or she wants.

What's more is that kids crave discipline and boundaries and need to understand that their toys need to put away at the end of the day. Not that if they aren't they will be punished. Boundaries are not a way of saying, "Do this, or you are in trouble." They are a way of saying, "Here is what is expected from you, please and thank you." It is an educational process, and one that can be enjoyed with your help.

Allow your child to determine how they want to put their toys away, and where they keep their favourites, as long as they put them away. Give them the latitude of creativity, and they will gladly expand their duties into exciting participation – instead of rebellion.

Discipline without Anger

Mindful parenting is simply extending your expectations to your child. For example, how would you like it if your boss marched into your office and screamed at you in anger because the report he wanted at noon is not on his desk? Terrible, perhaps? Now imagine how your child would feel if you disciplined them in a blind anger with yelling, angry words and an unacceptable tone. It would send them reeling, anxious and saddened by how you are treating them.

Keep in mind, there is very little that requires an angry approach, especially when you are dealing with children. How awful can it be? Did they paint your floor? Is it worth screaming about? Did they pour shampoo all over the bathtub? Hardly an uproarious event. In fact, there is very little that can happen in your child's life that is going to be solved through anger.

When you are upset with a situation, it is certainly okay to discipline your child. In fact, it is a must. However, the best course of action in either of the previous examples is to simply ask them to help you clean it up while you explain the damage or waste to the child during the process.

Anger can be hurtful, unnecessary and shortsighted, so take care not to damage your child's delicate senses by disciplining them in an unfair and biased manner simply because you have not learned to control your emotions.

Fences That Stretch and Those That Do Not

Much like it is always necessary for you to be aware that you are still the parent in this relationship; you must also determine which "fences", or boundaries, can bend and which cannot. As with any relationship, whether it is work, personal or romantic, there are "deal breakers" that you impose to make certain that your integrity is not overcome by your kindness. Children are no different. In fact, they are worse. Kids will push, push and push to see what they are able to get away with, so it is absolutely necessary to let them know what goes, and what does not.

Walking into the house with mud on your shoes? Not the worst offense ever. Just make sure they are responsible for cleaning up after themselves. Throwing items in the middle of a tantrum? Absolutely not. Again, as with any other relationship, you teach people how to treat you and your kids are absolutely not different. You should demand – through your mindful parenting, not through scolding and anger – that your child understands that being violent, hurtful or abusive is absolutely intolerable and will never be acceptable in any form. You can teach this by watching your own behavior and insuring that they never witness this type of negative outburst in your home, on television or in the movies. If it is inadvertently introduced to them – as you will absolutely find that you cannot shield them from everything – explain why it is wrong, and intolerable in a caring way.

It is important that your child respects the world around him, and everything that lives within it. This is possible by watching them carefully for any unsuspecting negative behavior, and teaching them the path of mindfulness. The best way, as it is with anything else, is to lead by example.

The Power of Good and Bad Choices

All parents want their kids to make good and positive choices so that they become amazing adults tomorrow, who will take conscious, intelligent decisions. When you offer choices to your kids it is important that you show compassion and kindness in whatever solutions you provide, while showing the same when they make their own decisions. Boost up your child's confidence by encouraging them in each of their efforts. Furthermore, it is crucial that parents do not indulge in comparing their children with others while scolding them. For instance, "Matt is such a great kid! Why can't you be more like Matt!?" Such comparisons can be quite damaging and may put your kid in a defensive position of complete despair. As a parent, it is your duty to guide your children in a calm and compassionate way while providing the support they need to succeed. If you provide the proper tools, trust and compassion, your kid will be able to do the rest.

The Reality of Enjoying Trying Versus Winning

Everyone around the world is so enamored with winning that it had disgusting levels, especially when it comes to parenting. You are an adult, who is raising a fragile, impressionable child, and you are trying to "beat" them at something? It's time to grow up. When you are a mindful parent, you understand that you and your child are traversing this crazy world together. You are in charge of guiding this small, impressionable person in making good decisions with the information that is available at the time. You are in charge of showing them wrong from right, without judgment or bias. Winning is not an option. Coaching, sharing, loving and providing a compassionate companion for them to lean on for support and guidance is the only goal you should have.

It is also important to know that it is impossible to get everything right. Just like your child, you are going to make the decisions before you with the best information you have available at the time. If it proves to be a bad decision, take responsibility for it and explain to your child how it was incorrect, and why you decided to do so to begin with. Kids are smarter than everyone thinks. They understand exactly what you are saying, when you say it. Do not insult their intelligence by avoiding the fact that they know your decision was a poor one. Explain why.

In this crazy world of parenting, the best anyone can do it try. Try, try and try again. Part of being a mindful parent is knowing that your kid is growing all the time, and that the challenges, celebrations, experiences and let downs are all going to follow you all into the future. Keep track of them, and learn from them together. You are both going to grow along the way, so enjoy it and be sure to keep learning and evolving with each other's needs.

൯ ൯ ൯

A truly rich man is one whose children run into his arms when his hands are empty.

- *Unknown*

൯ ൯ ൯

Made in the USA
San Bernardino, CA
13 October 2014